PAI

THE DC

GW00786613

PARTIES
THE DONE THING

Drusilla Beyfus
Cartoons by Austin

Ebury Press · London

Published in 1992 by Ebury Press
an imprint of Random House UK Limited
20 Vauxhall Bridge Road, London SW1V 2SA

Designed by Jason Shulman
Typeset in ITC Garamond
by Hope Services (Abingdon) Ltd
Printed in Great Britain
by Mackay of Chatham, PLC
Chatham, Kent

A catalogue record for this book is available from the
British Library.
ISBN 0 09 177009 2

To Jason

Contents

Preface

It would be thought very bad manners to add a line to a party invitation on how to behave but we may do so here without raising eyebrows.

Braving the odds against coming up with firm rules today, I have attempted to produce a few guidelines on some of the conundrums and dilemmas that arise out of giving a party or being a guest. In some respects, the areas of uncertainty have grown latterly as personal taste has such an influence on proceedings. An added complication is that the few signposts that do exist to prepare guests for what is in store are far from fail-safe. Even the description 'Informal' has many shades of meaning, depending on who, where and when. And you still may not guess correctly as to whether you can come as you are or should change.

Hosts, though free from the code that there is only one way to do things, have inherited a package of current concerns. Smoking tobacco, the drink/drive consideration and friends' food scruples are high on the agenda. Each calls for a tactful balance between hostly prerogative and guestly privilege that queries the assumption that anything goes.

The guest list is as much as ever the making of any party and, all depending, has wider scope. It may mix former spouses with present attachments, partners without each other, and women and walkers.

Timings show movement. The hour at which drinks parties begin and dinner is served has grown later, at least in the capital; groans by commuters, early risers and larks; relief by locals, late risers and owls.

Whereas in the case of a big do, notice of up to six weeks is far from unusual, the emphasis on planning ahead in general has had to adjust to pressure of work and the pitfalls of accepting an invitation when the weeks ahead are in a state of flux. For every dinner party that is forward planned there are scores of get-togethers with good food and drink and a well-laid table that spring into being with little notification. Apologies for this and that excess may abound but the one for 'short notice' is in limbo.

Excuses for declining have a new element. The number of receptions and balls given in aid of charity or good causes puts a premium on an acceptable excuse for declining. One such is to say that you have your own charity to support. Needless to add, it is a thoughtful gesture to send a small donation if you don't subscribe to the event.

Whether we like it or not, business and pleasure have become inextricably mixed at a proliferating number of sociable gatherings, from grand corporate entertaining to launches and charity lunches. These invitations pose the question of how far guests are expected to observe the courtesies that are usual at a private do, bearing in mind that they are expected to sing for their supper. An answer: the more personal the style of the arrangements the greater the onus on guests to credit the hosts with generous motives and to do the proper thing. At a business-oriented do, business practice usually applies.

Whatever the occasion, one unchanging rule is that first impressions should be the pleasure of the giver in his or her own party.

Non-party

When is a party not a party? Some have a ready answer. It is the occasion when the inviter prefaces their invitation with the remark, 'It is not really a party.'

Now to confuse matters: there are occasions that fulfil all the criteria of a party that may be announced in this deprecating fashion. But there are also gatherings that fit the disclaimer.

It is these we are concerned with here. The non-party has an honoured place in the pantheon of entertaining. These are jolly occasions that blow up unannounced and consist of a few friends and perhaps family too, and are essentially last-minute affairs. Yet oddly enough, many non-party givers and goers will testify that they had some of the nicest times they can remember at these occasions. It is fact that spontaneous hospitality is often remembered more fondly than many a premeditated

Heavens! We left the baby on that bed.

gathering at which the host has taken pains to roll out the red carpet.

The explanation is probably quite simple. Everyone expects less, the surprise element are persuasive and nobody present feels bound to perform onerous hostly or guestly duties. Another reason is the way they come into being.

A collective approach comes into its own as often as not and food and drink and shopping are partly shared. The way it works is the way it works for you by definition but usually the number one giver does the asking, provides the space and most of the food whilst leaving others to fill the gaps, bring some of the drink and help out generally. Not even a non-party can survive without someone to head it and be prepared to do the better part of the organising.

A collective party shares costs and eases the workload of the principal host, and those who retire from a day's hard toil with the task of entertaining a few friends at home are likely to greet with relief the prospect of a job if not done then half done. Guests who contribute to the occasion do not expect to be reimbursed as a rule.

The party at which guests provide much of the hospitality can be applied to picnics of all kinds and with management can work for quite formal gatherings. A bride and bridegroom known to the writer who were pushed for pence managed to organise a successful wedding reception for themselves along these lines.

One reminder: guests bringing dishes to eat in their own containers usually do want to have these returned. Best to clean and hand back before they leave, all else being equal, and the deed is done.

A box at Ascot

The party in a private box at Royal Ascot often consists of two parties: the serious punters who are absorbed in their chances of winning the 2.30 and those who go for the social side, the fashion stakes and the champagne. Added to the former may be race-goers who take their

I brought them to spot celebrities.

racing seriously but who don't care to bet.

Royal Ascot breeds great loyalty amongst its supporters who have been joined latterly by many first-timers brought in on a wave of corporate hospitality.

Somehow, all these various members have to come to an accommodation in a fairly confined space as far as the box is concerned. Boxes in the main grandstand enjoy a close and uninterrupted view of the race course and the passing motley. Each contains a few seats, a table and a television set that relays the events from beginning to end.

Good advice for the sociable is to leave the punters to

their deliberations undisturbed, once racing is in the offing. They will probably play their part during lunch before the races start and afterwards.

Race-goers whose tolerance of horse racing and betting is somewhat limited find other distractions and amusements. They talk amongst themselves, explore the scene outside, study the fashion form and probably observe observers. One of the attractions in between races is to stroll over to the saddling enclosure where some of the finest flat racing horses to be bred can be seen as they are led round the ground. The Queen is often amongst the witnesses.

Dressing for the occasion remains part and parcel of the day for both sexes. Among the women, there is always a contingent that is flamboyantly or freakily attired but the generality of Ascotites put on their best with a bonnet. Hats and gloves go hand in hand. Male guests in the boxes may wear lounge suits but the overwhelming proportion of them are clad in morning dress and toppers, most likely hired for the occasion. Dress codes at this level are less restrictive than for the Royal Enclosure where those who are 'improperly dressed' are not admitted.

Depending on the generosity of your host (or his or her company), hospitality for guests in private boxes includes lunch with several courses, served in some style with china plates and dinner-table knife and forkery. The party is waited upon, champagne and wines flow liberally throughout the day. Teatime sees the arrival of traditional tuck, strawberries and cream and more champagne is served. At tea, with some races to go, the talk is of winners and losers, punters versus bookies, and the miraculous and unexpected events that are part of a race-goer's mythology.

The occasion opens with the familiar scene of members of the royal family being driven down the race course in their landaus, escorted by uniformed outriders. As there is usually some competition amongst the party to get a good view of the scene and the subsequent races, anyone who can gain an advantageous position without seeming to be pushy, has won one race. However, all the outdoor events can be seen on the television set indoors.

As betting predominates, it may be worth mentioning that no guest is likely to be thought the less of if they do not wish to gamble their readies. As well, even among those who are placing large bets, it may be a point for novices that the smallest bet will be gobbled up by the bookies. Experienced punters have their cash or a credit card at the ready as business is brisk.

Tips may be begged from fellow punters but people should not be put off if the pro is unwilling to produce one. Some don't like the idea of taking the risk of being associated with a friend's loss. The atmosphere is one in which winners are warmly congratulated, with special recognition accorded to those whose win was picked with a pin. Losers, as usual, are expected to bear their pain with fortitude – at least in public.

A thank-you letter to the host is a must. Those who can't call on the day's tally for a suitable comment might draw on the physical beauty of the setting and the visual charm of the races – points appreciated by artists over the decades.

Surprisingly . . .

The party that comes as a big surprise to the guest of honour is having a long innings. Encouraged by the vein of secrecy and pretence involved, not to speak of its theatricality, the ruse has been known to appeal to even jaded palates. The leading man or lady is likely to be touched by the thought not only of the party itself but that everyone was so cunning. Guests have the pleasure of congratulating themselves on keeping the secret despite all.

Any excuse will do but the party is associated with major anniversaries and other milestones. The way arrangements go is for the host to canvass guests with as much discretion as can be summoned. Invitation cards, for example, are eschewed in favour of less conspicuous forms such as letters, telephone calls and word of mouth. Acceptances are expected to be similarly circumspect in execution.

*Thank heavens we gave the slip to those
bores from the office.*

Of course the notion is childlike, but that is half the fun. Unfair play is for any of the participants not to pay attention or to be blasé and give the game away.

More than usually important for guests is a punctual arrival. The full dramatic impact is contained in the first few seconds as the guest of honour arrives (lured to the occasion through some alibi). And as he or she steps innocently into the fray, there are all these good people. Honours to those who can feign wonder.

It may be worth mentioning that not everyone desires to see their biography unfold unbidden before their eyes. Some might even shudder at the thought.

6.30 pm
Drinks

Drinks parties divide the punters into two camps: those who go and those who despise the invitation and go.

The classic case in favour is the promise of the unknown: you are never quite sure whom you might bump into. And to look at the matter cold bloodedly, the occasion represents an efficient use of an hour or so, bearing in mind the numbers of people that you may meet, greet, say hello to, as well as the possibility of renewing old friendships and perhaps founding new ones.

As well, the escape clauses are appealing. You can come early or late within reason, there is little risk of getting stuck with someone uncongenial as at a dinner party table, and you may slope off without announcing the fact to the host or hostess. In addition, there's the flexibility of being able to bring along an uninvited friend.

From a party-giver's viewpoint, the notion of swooshing a gaggle of friends, acquaintances, must-haves and long-neglected allies into one room for a couple of hours or so with drink and canapés only is a practical way of repaying hospitality at a blow. The crowd, the atmosphere and the drink will conspire to swallow any awkward cusses or persons with whom a long evening at dinner would be a distinct downer.

Hosts who wish to invite VIPs and grandees often find they have better luck in netting their guests of honour with an invitation to a drinks party than with one to a premeditated dinner party. The flexibility of arrangements means the sought-after can accept for drinks on the basis that they will come if commitments permit, without feeling they are incommoding the host.

As to whom not to put on the guest list, it is worth mentioning the experience of one who is well known for her big parties. She tries to avoid inviting husbands and former wives on the same night, or leading men and leading ladies who do not get along. The consequences of organising serial entertainments have taught her that 'giving three parties is not three times more difficult than giving one.'

Kind hosts ensure that new arrivals are introduced to a few people who might like to meet them and take pains to avoid jettisoning them into the throng without first settling them with someone friendly to talk to. The hostly task is to circulate and make sure that people who would like to get together, do, or those whom they think should be brought within orbit of each other, are. Having time for everybody is part of the art.

Among guestly skills is knowing how to escape a bore when honesty deters them from uttering the usual excuse, 'Well, I mustn't keep you from the others.' After

Oh dear. Henry's trying to liven things up.

a respectable interval has elapsed it is not impolite to say that you intend to circulate, nor to mention, by way of a get-away, that you want to talk to So and So before they leave. A cocktail party consists of ebb and flow, mix and mingle, rather like low tide on a seashore. Tributaries merge and separate and reform new patterns. Part of it is breaking up groups. A natural break in the conversation is usually offered when someone else comes over to say hello to you or the person with whom you have been conversing. If a parting gesture is needed, the leaver may always say, 'It was very good to meet you,' or some such sentiment.

Hangers-on for a last glass are endemic at most drinks parties. Getting them to go within the bounds of tact requires a firm move. Calling a halt to the drink may not do the trick. Opening windows and letting in a cold blast of air has been known to move somnolent bodies swiftly but this is a seasonal ploy, as is turning down the lights. The announcement by the hosts that they are off to dinner elsewhere and have to lock up may sound graceless but it works.

Company beano

Office parties are easy to give but difficult to pull off successfully. A strain of 'must-haves' and 'must-do's' tends to quell the party spirit along with the omnipresent awareness that you must mind your P's and Q's.

What can animate the occasion is putting some special effort and imagination into the planning and organisation. Somehow a group of people who have been in each other's orbit for many long days has to be transmuted into a sociable throng newly energised by the hospitality.

The giver of the party is the key, as usual. Men or women who play this one most effectively focus on the host side of the role, with the company heavyweight guise worn lightly.

One practical measure is to take the trouble to find an interesting place or spot where the jolly can take place. It gets people out of the familiar working environment and shows willing – the option could he historic, beautiful, quirky or entertaining. In the case of small numbers, the gathering could take place at wherever is home to the host or an associate – an invitation that is usually greatly appreciated.

A similar approach might work wonders with the food and drink as hospitality at these do's has no great reputation for innovation. No-one is suggesting rare delicasies or expensive tipple, but even a half decent choice of wine would indicate consideration.

The guest list can present dilemmas except when the all-in policy applies, as at the typical Christmas party. On other occasions, the response to being left out is easier to bear if some logic can be seen to apply to the selection of guests – perhaps bosses should take note. The answer to the question of whether an employee can ask to be included in the party, within the bounds of politeness, is probably no – a caveat that would apply at any private occasion.

To return to our boss-as-host. It is friendly if he or she can welcome everyone individually, assuming numbers make this a practicable gesture. In any case, mixing and mingling is of the essence as the office party is one of the few official occasions when distances between members if not banished are bridged. Most employees entertain the idea of having a private word with the boss. In turn, bosses can exercise their prerogative of giving praise where a raise is due.

Guests too are enjoined to circulate and to desist, at least for a while, from the tendency to reconstitute the

*The office party is the continuation of office
politics by other means.*

coteries and groupings that belong to the workplace.
Little knots of persons virtually continuing the business
of the day may serve the department in question but
doesn't say partying to anyone.

An incentive for party members to mingle is the
knowledge that at a sociable do the hierarchy is not what
it is, and lesser mortals can button-hole, beard and open
conversations with one and all. At the company dance or
knees-up, it's almost bad form for guests and hosts to
partner their peers only.

Suggesting appropriate topics for conversation
between a member of staff and a big wig whom they
scarcely know is unproductive in this context. What can

be said is that, in general, bosses like to hear something to their advantage in one form or another and they do appreciate loyalty and enthusiasm.

Cynics claim that flatterers do best in these exchanges and, as a judgment, it can be hard to disprove. However, brown-nosing is particularly conspicuous on such an occasion and woe betide anyone who subsequently falls into the hands of abstainers.

Conversation may or may not play a part in the much-aired topic of louche behaviour between the sexes on this occasion. Office parties in general are probably rather correct in this respect, or so it may be surmised, but exceptions have cast an aura of sexual licence over the whole engagement.

It is clearly discourteous for a man to make assumptions about a woman's willingness to comply with his advances, and doubly so if the lady has the disadvantage of being junior to him in status. The imbalance in their relative standing compromises her freedom to tell him to push off. Women may help themselves, though; as a start, they could dress in a manner that hits a mean between business-like formality and strutting their stuff.

What the office party has going for it is that everyone likes to be thanked for their efforts, which is the point of the occasion. As well, the mixture has on its side the promise of shop talk, the gossip on the grapevine, news of local mischief, as well the opportunity of doing yourself a bit of good. It could be fun – well stage managed.

*We invited him because in black tie he looks
like a bouncer.*

Dress decoded

What to wear at a party is a question with the widest
range of acceptable answers in living memory. Arguable
as this case may be, it is hardly a big help to anyone pon-
dering on whether to go for short or long or wear a
polo-neck with a dinner jacket.

It is worth mentioning at the outset that anything
absolutely never goes. Despite the general relaxation of
dress codes at almost every kind of do, little has changed

the rule that there are clothes horses for courses. Some choices will always seem more at home than others. The prospect of being overdressed is nearly equalled in potential embarrassment by the thought of failing to don Sunday Best when all about you are well attired.

What adds to the hazards of giving advice is that those categories of attire that would once be proscribed – such as, for women, exposed female underpinnings, or for either sex, sports or working gear, for example – have upturned etiquette and become part of fashion's options. Even the dictum that men should remove headgear when indoors has been eased. Acceptability depends on the style of the garment and on the manner in which it is worn as much as anything. One could say that what makes dress improper is the wearer him or herself.

Constant amidst the confusion are those imprecise phrases that party-givers utter by way of signalling their wishes to friends about what to wear. As shades of meaning alter with the times, the code could be unscrambled along these lines.

'Come as you are' is to be treated with circumspection. Best to put a flattering interpretation on what the host assumes you might be wearing. A mangy sweater and shredded jeans is doubtful – unless you wish to teach the speaker a lesson.

'Don't bother to change' is a manner of speech. Knowing house rules is the only surefire way of interpreting the edict. Anyone who mentions changing very probably has in mind party-ish clothes: jacket and collar and neck-tie (or smart tieless equivalent) for men, clothes which pay respect to the occasion for women.

'Jack is putting on black-tie' doesn't mean necessarily that all the men will be dressed as penguins but indicates a status of attire such as smoking jackets, bow-ties, polo-necks with dinner jackets, fancy waistcoats and other forms of plumage. Black-tie encourages women to put on their finery, which may be short or long, now an irrelevant demarcation line.

The time

The connection between the hour at which guests are invited, and the likely level of hospitality, is no longer the guideline that it once was. Some timings have been floated off from their erstwhile certainties, and other stated hours remain quite attached to their own customs. For example, in the capital an invitation to a reception at 7 pm might mean a splendid repast at some stage during the evening but, in the absence of any other information, equally well might mean that the guest was expected to eat beforehand or afterwards.

A rough-and-ready translation of arrival times considered in relation to hostly intentions, might go around

She's rather dictatorial, but her parties run on time.

the o'clocks of hospitality like this.

8 am–10 am: breakfast, mixing eggs and egos

10 am–2 pm (ish): brunch without any pretensions about providing a menu with the 'L' as in lunch, together with alcoholic beverages

12 noon–1.30 pm: drinks with no more than a nod towards Tum

12.30 pm–2.30 pm: as before, with the possibility of more than a token nod towards Tum

12.30 pm for 1 pm: indubitably, lunch

1 pm for 1.15 pm: as before

3.45 pm or 4 pm: tea and teatime accompaniments with the chance of the offer of a jar before leaving

5 pm: high tea, perhaps with a cooked dish. In some parts of the country 'tea' is the main meal of the day.

6 pm–8 pm: surefire drinks with the chance of canapés

6.30 pm–8.30 pm: as before

7 pm–9 pm: drinks with the chance of one up from canapés

7 pm–10 pm: as before (unless otherwise stated)

7.45 pm for 8 pm, 8 pm for 8.15 pm and 8 pm for 8.30 pm: definitely dinner

9.30 pm or 10 pm: after-dinner drinks with the possibility of a morsel or two to eat (unless supper is indicated). If the given hour is for a dance or ball – hot breakfast dishes and champagne before the finale.

Disguised in this account is the ambiguous part played by canapés, which can mean a few sparse nuts and crisps, or in good hands may be a culinary feast, albeit, bite sized. The previously mentioned category, one up from canapés, suggests that with luck, you can virtually dine off the offerings. And, by the same token, hosts who provide imaginative and satisfying canapés can feel they are playing fair by the appetites of their guests.

Notwithstanding improvement in the standard of morsel-and-munch, canny hosts are adopting means of clarifying what their friends can expect on the house, through spelling out the facts. For example, at an anniversary party, the invitation might state, 'Reception 7 pm'; 'Dinner 8.15 pm'. The wording makes clear that guests are invited to dine, which a mention of 'Reception' alone fails to make clear and also tips off those who choose to attend the reception only that they are expected to hop it before the announced hour of dinner.

A word about much of the practice described. Readers will recognise that this has an urban, not to say metropolitan, edge. In country parts, sociable hours and the host's intentions tend to remain as once they were. Also, where distance is a consideration, hospitable hosts try to ensure that their guests can count on the welcome of good food and drink. Bearing in mind the general uncertainty, is it then in order for an invitee to ask, for example, whether a hot dinner is in the offing? Not really, as kind guests take what comes their way without probing.

Bottle bearing

To bring or not to bring a bottle to the party exercises the minds of guests who don't feel wholly on familiar ground. They may wonder whether the offering will be appreciated or thought inappropriate. Then again, there is the unworthy speculation as to whether they can get away with arriving empty handed at an occasion when others have elected to come bearing vinous gifts.

What has a bearing is the standing of the bringer in relation to the host, and the nature of the occasion. In general, first timers, those who are invited by people who are largely unknown to them or whose standards of hospitality are only guessed at, do well to think twice before opting to bring a bottle. Other occasions might be when the invitation comes from a host who is self-evidently senior to the guest.

Not forgetting that 'no man wishes to insult his host by bringing a bottle' – to paraphrase Thackeray – the risk lies in the host's reaction that the gesture is superfluous. They may hold to the view that they prefer to be the sole providers, or that an unacceptable level of intimacy is implied by the gesture. Some of the old school do genuinely dislike accepting presents from people they don't know in all cases.

A general rule is that in nine instances out of ten, and as between friends at a private do, the gesture will be found more than acceptable. Wine buffs will be especially gratified by an interesting choice of bottle. However, it is by no means an obligation to bring, with the exception of announced bottle parties.

The decision to produce an offering has its own puzzles. One is the familiar situation in which a helper at the door who is not the intended recipient offers to take charge of the offering. Fine, but should you mention the existence of the present to the host or is it better to hang on to your prize and answer the question by handing it in person? An added consideration may be that handing over in front of the assembled party, may or may not, unwittingly cause discomfiture to those who arrived empty handed. Most convenient, at least, is to allow the helper to organise things and to reserve the right to be the first to tell the host that a bottle or two awaits them for later.

Producing an offering of a bottle of champagne, ready chilled, sounds like a great idea, which in most cases it proves to be. However, where the recipient has champagne tastes but perhaps lacks the wherewithal to support them, the gesture could be better thought of. It may be that a solo bottle is insufficient for the numbers involved and cracking it will highlight the house's inability or unwillingness to top up the round. Also, the host may consider that the gesture requires champagne glasses for all and these too may be in short supply. Where all else is equal, it goes without saying that a present of a primed bottle of bubbly kick starts the occasion.

Nevertheless, the recipient is well within limits if he or she elects to ignore the hint and carries the loot away to some bourne from which there is no intention of returning it until any threat of having to share a drop in company has long passed. That's what presents are for.

It is worth mentioning that it is not considered polite, regretably, for a giver to refer to the existence of the bottle if it remains uncorked, and the table appears to have run dry. The present disappears into the limbo of hostly prerogatives and cannot be reclaimed by the giver – if propriety is to be minded.

As a present of a bottle is a form of thank you in

advance the question arises as to whether it is not a substitute for a bread-and-butter letter? Doubtful to a definite no.

This seems the place to mention that wine has many points in favour as a celebratory present, beyond the token party gesture. Wine comes into its own as a wedding offering, especially in the instance of a couple who have already set up home, or those who are marrying again and are queasy about a second wedding list. Alternatively, a couple who are down on their luck might be cheered by the prospect of pouring a decent glass of the grape.

Admittedly, wine is sometimes criticised as an impersonal choice but this can be got round by the giver making a knowledgable match between bottle and imbiber.

Sociable baby

At a big drinks party, the baby was parked at a remove from the gathering. The mother made repeated visits to check on her infant. The father, mildly piqued by his wife's continual absences from proceedings, asked what was the matter? 'Someone might take him,' she replied, defensively. 'Who on earth,' parried the male parent, 'would want to nick a baby?' Heartless maybe, but individuals have different values when it comes to taking a

*Should we have made it a
'bring-a-bottle' party?*

baby along to drinks or dinner.

Parents have a wish to take their babies to every kind of social gathering and, as a consequence, adjustments have to be made all round. There are many parties to be considered: the youngest member in question, the parents, the hosts and the other guests.

Generally, inviters of those with a baby in arms or a toddler in tow, do the polite thing if they ask if their friends would like to bring their young. It is worth mentioning that even if the extended invitation is declined, the thought will rate.

A partisan word about weekends. The time is child-led

for many professionals and others who employ child-carers during weekdays but who have their offspring to themselves at the week's end. An invitation to a Saturday-night dinner party or Sunday lunch stands a better chance of acceptance if baby can come too. A bonus for hosts is knowing that their friends won't have to go to the trouble and expense of hiring a baby-sitter with the concomitant obligation to ensure that the investment yielded due rewards.

Is it considered courteous to ask if one may bring the baby? Dubious, if the hosts are Old Britain. One strategy might be to mention baby-sitting difficulties in the hopes of evincing a positive response. If none is forthcoming, recommendations are against asking a favour. If a host is sticky on the subject, chances are that the request doesn't fit in, for one reason or another.

When the infant accompanies the parents, hosts are expected to ask what arrangements would suit. The usual spot for occupation is the hostess's bedroom – an early privilege if you like. Babies in arms may well settle but toddlers often prefer to stay closer to their parents.

It is almost always sound practice for a parent to bring a few favoured playthings for their babies or tots. These help to break the ice and may offer some respite to adults in the search for ideas to amuse the youngest member – a must-bring in childless households especially and moreover, may save the house breakables.

When the baby is having a bad day and cries inconsolably, some parents take the view that this is all part of sharing the development of a new human being, and continue to tuck into their polenta and wild mushrooms, largely unconcerned. Others of a more sensitive nature will think it time to go home. Few hosts who have gone to some trouble to entertain their friends will wish their efforts to be remembered for squalls and hushabyes.

The baby may be at the breast – still an issue in mixed company. In general on this point, votes go to the mother who nurses with decorum, and who also bothers to ask her host or hostess where she may attend to her baby. An acceptable approach might be: amongst females, go ahead without a second thought; amongst close friends irrespective of gender, proceed with an eye to the guest list; amongst members of the opposite sex whose reactions can only be surmised, withdrawing is the safe bet.

Bread before cake

Many people brought up on a diet of English table manners would rather die than eat a slice of chocolate cake before accepting a slice of bread and butter at the tea table. Undeniably, standards have deteriorated in the wake of grazing and the fad for snatching bites of this and that in public. Nevertheless, an awareness of the

*I'm afraid something's come up at the
last minute.*

importance of minding your P's and Q's at table remains
a litmus test of savoir-faire, said to be felt particularly
by the uninitiated. In favour of the English way is effi-
ciency, by and large. As well, the accepted rules pay
attention to the susceptibilities of any neighbour or
spectator.

Hard lines of correctitude have long since bitten the
dust and whatever a person might think to themselves,
few would be likely to denigrate someone with the old
epithet that he or she 'didn't know how to handle a knife
and fork'. The truth is that some forms of the established
code can be infringed with impunity as a general rule
whereas other solecisms suggest you really should know
better. The following attempts to distinguish t'other
from which at a dinner party.

PERMISSIBLE LAPSES:

Tucking in before the hostess gives the word
Putting elbows on the table
Asking for a taster from a neighbour's plate
Helping yourself uninvited to the wine on the table
Lifting green salad onto the main-course plate and
   ignoring the purpose-laid one
Sprinkling the salt and pepper over your food
Stretching for the butter dish or the sauce boat
Passing on the pudding course
Eating fresh fruit in the fingers
Producing your own sweetener for coffee or tea
Remarking on the food

IMPERMISSIBLE LAPSES:

Holding the handle of a knife like a pencil
Cutting up meat into 'a dog's dinner'
Drinking out of the bottle
Trading places
Forgetting to pass the port
Throwing bread rolls
Filching the last cream bun without offering it first
Leaning back on fragile chairs
Filling your own glass without attending to a
   neighbour's
Producing a mobile telephone
Dirty hands

Bringing your own diet rations (without previous consultation with the host)
Yawning, belching, noisy nose-blowing and zzzing off
Not complimenting the cook

Bread before cakes and such edicts apply equally to both sexes but much else in the book of table manners is shaped by sex distinction, lapses not excluded. Old-fashioned politeness is for the male to pull out a chair for the woman to be seated comfortably, to be attentive to both his female neighbours and never to turn his back upon a woman. It goes without saying that for a male to play footsie without any sign of reciprocation is asking for rejection.

Courtesy is for women to share their company with both neighbours, to refrain from hogging the favourite and to observe this rule in the case of a member of their own sex. If the occasion is one of the few at which the women are expected to withdraw and to leave the men to themselves and the port, it would be ungracious to remain seated to say the least. On the other hand, for the men to protract the phase of separation beyond a token break seems unmannerly.

The offer to lend a hand if the hosts are managing all the work is obligatory, and applies to members of both sexes. However, should the gesture be declined, guests are advised to relax and enjoy being waited upon, mindful that it will be their turn next time.

I'm pairing off bores with good listeners.

Irregular number

The guest list is not what it was by a long shot. Many conventions have given way to a more relaxed approach on such topics as equal numbers at the dinner party, asking members of a couple, being a single, female host.

Shaken certainties pose new uncertainties in some areas. The seated dinner party as the most structured form of entertaining is an arena where any alteration in the equal distribution of the sexes is most visible. The picture of a grand dinner party as a group of penguins evenly interspersed with persons in pearls is very much with us but even dinner jackets no longer guarantee the old order.

What is acceptable, then, when one of a couple is

unable to accept? Usually hosts do the decent thing and extend the invitation to him or her alone. If they think it unlikely they will be able to raise a member of the opposite sex as a substitute dinner-party partner, it might be an idea to say so in advance so the guest knows what not to expect as it were.

Incidentally, on this point, hesitancy surrounds whether the one of the couple who can accept can ask if they may come or have to wait until the host formally invites them in their own right. Since it is well within limits for the party-giver to withdraw the invitation on the grounds of equal numbers, asking may be premature. Hosts who exercise this prerogative usually temper the decision by saying that they hope that both of you can come next time.

If guests of the same sex are to be seated beside one another at a mixed party, some hosts take the view that it is a nice idea to give them a place of honour as their neighbour, irrespective of gender. Another point of consideration is for the party-giver to choose a specially interesting member of the opposite sex to be placed beside the one who has someone of his or her own gender as the other neighbour.

An interjection at this point. Airing such issues may have an almost Edwardian quality to some. But the intimacy of a dinner party, like theatre, is bound by its own artifices and conventions that include the custom of mixing the sexes evenly at table. If things are to be different, polite hosts make an attempt to reassure anyone who might be feeling the odd man out.

Cross-overs between work and play produce their own dilemmas. For instance, is it acceptable for an associate to invite his or her married workmate to dine without including the latter's spouse in the proposal? Very doubtful, put like that. One of the few surviving props of matrimony in society is that marriage means you are invited as a couple. A possible strategy within the limits of politeness would be to arrange what might be described euphemistically as a working lunch.

The question of the equal distribution of sexes can be a teaser for single women as hosts. It is certainly no good reason for retiring from the scene. If the boyfriend isn't available, or she doesn't have a boyfriend or her address book is short on single sociable males, the tendency is to manage without a male deputed to act as a co-host, and to rise above irregular numbers. Walkers increasingly fill the bill at formal do's when equal numbers are *de rigueur*.

Gay guests and friends may have to be considered if thinking of partners in relation to equal numbers. The accepted form at a structured dinner party is to alternate men and women in the usual way.

Obviously, many of these points fade into insignificance at a drinks party or at a buffet lunch or dinner as small disparities in the gender count of the guests are far less apparent. If the gathering is to be predominantly or even exclusively female, is there any need to mention the fact? Surely not, except in cases where the host considers her female friends might be disconcerted by an absence of escorts. Worth a mention in this connection is that men's long-standing right to enjoy their own company is extended to members of the opposite sex without disparagement.

The *Zeitgeist* encourages a more open-minded approach to the eligibility of guests without overturning the works. People are invited because of themselves and on grounds of personal liking, rather than on account of their marital status, gender or sexual orientation. Admittedly, this criterion may be just as discriminatory as the old code of exclusion (spouses and partners may languish uninvited) but it does give prospective guests a better chance to be judged on their own merits.

However, harbingers of social change tend to get their comeuppance as patterns die hard. Therefore, none of the foregoing should be read as suggesting that life won't go on as before. At many a table, the host will take his place at the head and announce, 'Chris, will you sit over here next to Lucy?' And if custom is to be followed, Lucy takes it on the chin with a smile.

An unamended rule about the guest list – whoever this may consist of – concerns who is not on it. Those who have a reasonable expectation of being asked to the party and who are left out are liable to turn into elephants and never forget.

Food scruples

Wondering whether the people round the table will get on has to some degree been supplanted by speculation as to whether everyone's food tastes will be compatible. Acknowledging the other's food proscriptions and prohibitions has become more than a formal factor in entertaining, and affects guest list, menu and chat, alike.

Since people are feisty about their food beliefs it is in the interests of the future of hospitality to find ways in which dissenters can sit down with confidence with mainstream eaters.

Probably the most widely shared experience is that in which a carnivorous household entertains a committed vegetarian. Questions arise as to how the cook can do right by his or her veggie guest without turning the meal into a penance for others. And where does the non-meat eater draw the line in imposing his or her views on those who love tucking into a steak?

Thoughtful providers try to take account of their friend's embargoes whilst bearing in mind that others present may not enjoy a wholly vegetarian cuisine. The usual way is to produce side dishes or accompaniments to a dish that will be to the liking of lone wolf, reserving the main dish for majority tastes.

The prevalence of pasta dishes and recipes from many ethnic cuisines that do not depend on meat as an ingre-

If nature intended us to be herbivores how come she gave us these teeth?

dient and that are appreciated by meat eaters and non-meat eaters alike, makes the task of the cook a little less daunting and demanding.

During the course of the meal, whoever is serving should refrain from giving the abstainer a helping of some proscribed ingredient on the basis of maintaining the appearance of unity and the assumption that they may leave what they do not like. For many committed vegetarians, a helping of meat on their plate is enough to quench their appetites.

Most vegetarians respond to this situation by eating whichever part of the meal is to their liking, and having established their views ahead of time, give the remainder a miss with the connivance of the host. If they hold hard-line views and carnivorous fare is seriously distasteful to them, there is a valid argument in favour of declining the invitation or of the host suggesting another date to which the like-minded could be rallied.

Concessions by the cultist may also be called for if the talk gets round to food scruples. Lobbyists or those of that ilk are advised to go easy on the blood and guts of the argument. The company may be put off their fare by a graphic account of slaughter-house methods or a clinical dissection of hormonal additives to farm stock. Notwithstanding the purpose of the exercise, what has to be borne in mind is that a dinner table is more than a platform for proselytisers whose message undermines the spirit of the occasion.

Hosts, on the other hand, are asked to forgo any temptation to pooh pooh their guests' beliefs as mere food faddery. They are liable to be reminded of the impressive number of non-meat eaters in our midst who have taken to the path on moral or health grounds or both.

Respecting the food codes of others is as old as hospitality itself, rooted in religious and cultural distinctions. Yet, the current outcrop of food cults has to be accepted unless the shared table is to be fatally disrupted and we eat only in a gastronomical ghetto. Cooking probably holds the key to a multi-cultural approach – the mantra is diversity within togetherness. Certainly, much business and official partying has accepted the two-tier menu. Is it in order then for a non-meat eater to check in advance? Yes, in all probability, save at very grand do's.

*I'm Mary Brown. Mrs. Alfred Jones is my
professional name.*

Married names

So far there is no completely satisfactory answer to the conundrum of how to introduce a female spouse who is known professionally by a name other than her married one. That is, there is no way that satisfies all the parties concerned equally.

In the meantime, we all muddle through along these lines. Enter the female spouse with a double credit. The first doubt to assail the host is the preference of the lady in question. Does she prefer to sail under her husband's colours in private life, or might she be miffed if introduced with a handle that denies her professional identity or status?

A further consideration occurs in those cases in which the guest's work carries with it some degree of public recognition. Is it not rough on the other guests to have Marsha Fernley, who might be known to them as the recording harpist, or the manager of a local business or who is the live wire up at the clinic, introduced under her anonymous guise as the wife of Jack Walker? The intelligence could spark a conversational lead, or at least provide a forewarning in sensitive situations about what not to say.

No mention has been made yet of the husband's viewpoint. A cavalier omission of the existence of the marital tie in public may touch off all manner of buried resentments. Does one of the outward symbols of marriage count for nought? Is she not his to have and to hold and to bear his name? These are amongst the more extreme reactions that may be unleashed, this notwithstanding husbandly pride in his wife's achievements.

What usually happens is for the introducer to canvas the wife's opinion, thus, 'Do you like to be Marsha Fernley or Mrs Jack Walker?' The advantage of this approach is that it mentions both names in one breath. So far so good. But alas, it may only work once as in all probability the host will follow the recommended line in subsequent introductions.

The guest in the case is now called upon to declare her wishes, which she is free to do, unequivocally. Many women, though, prefer to demur and say something along the lines that they really don't mind or that either will serve, thus leaving the ball in the court of the person making the introduction. A measure adopted by many women with double handles is to use whichever identity corresponds to the interests of their conversationalist and suits the occasion.

Should few opportunities present themselves to the host for taking the pulse of the guest with a dual appellation, he or she may rely on etiquette. It is at least correct to introduce a woman under her married name except when a professional audience knows her under another and she is attending as a member of her chosen profession or business.

Those who wait

Only the most optimistic or inexperienced of party-givers would be surprised by unpunctual guests. The art of the host, as usual, is to stage manage proceedings in a manner that minimises any discomfiture and smooths over any potential awkwardness. This may take some doing as the guest who fails to materialise, paradoxically, may be more of a presence than those who turn up. What with the likelihood of speculation about the absentee's possible whereabouts, a character sketch as to his or her habit of always being on the dot or invariably turning up late,

*Apparently he's a famous astronomer with
very unusual ideas about time.*

and an open discussion about whether to hang on a bit
in hope or to proceed as planned, the tardy cast a long
shadow over all proceedings and plans.

At a sit-down dinner or lunch, absentee guests are
more conspicuous than at a buffet, which may touch off
the mini-debate referred to. The means may be demo-
cratic but it tends to put the pro-feeders in an invidious
position by allowing the wait-a-whilers to occupy the gra-
cious ground.

It is the role of the host to lead and, as it is his or her
prerogative to decide on the shape of the occasion, it is
certainly within limits to keep to a given timetable.

Exactly how long a host is prepared to wait until the
party is complete depends on whether delay fits in with
everyone else's arrangements and, of course, on the state
of the cooking. A leeway of about fifteen minutes post
the hour at which people would usually sit down to

dine, seems fair – some would say generous.

At table, it might seem churlish immediately to whisk away the absent guest's place-setting. More hospitable is to allow him or her the benefit of the doubt for the first course. Hosts are also obliged to spare a thought for the absentee's neighbours at table who are inevitably deprived of company. As and when the eating irons for the guest are cleared away, people move to close up.

Unholy smoke

Balancing a smoker's rights with those of the anti's is a particularly delicate issue at a private do. The prerogatives of hosts and the privileges of guests are rarely poised in such sharp conflict as when the party-giver frowns on smoking and the guest fancies a ciggie or a pipe of tobacco.

What may be done to cause the least offence? Despite support for banning the weed in public places, the onus in private remains on hosts to forewarn unwary smokers that they do not permit smoking. Such tactics at least prepare the guest for what may be in store and also produces a bona fide excuse for declining. Whether the guest should mention the embargo as the reason is debatable in certain circumstances. To do so might suggest a wild addiction to tobacco, which might or might not be applicable. Furthermore, the truth might be less

dramatic, but equally problematic as an excuse. The guest might just feel put-upon and deprived of the pleasure of his or her habit. A case for a fib.

On the occasion of a big party, the idea has been floated of announcing 'No smoking' on invitations. If this is to be the case, it seems fair warning. But as a means it might be thought to have an officious air. A way round that has been known to work in cases where there are numbers and the space is to designate separate areas – one for the puffers, the other to be kept as a smokeless zone.

Guests are inevitably on the receiving end of their host's attitudes towards smoking but they are entitled to

45

have their predilections considered. They have on their side that hosts who impose their own whims and wishes on their guests are on thin ice when it comes to criticising others for ignoring the prohibition. Some give-and-take on the matter might assume the following form.

Guests who accept invitations with the no-smoking caveat are obliged to keep the pact if they wish to be thought polite. If the appeal of their habit calls, they should be prepared to take their smoke outside. If they were unaware of the embargo, the householder who insisted on his or her guests retiring to smoke, would surely be entering the realms of black hostmanship. Non-smokers out and about in the territories of confirmed smokers are obliged to accept the position with as good a grace as they can muster.

Smoking at table has always been discouraged as tobacco fumes blunt the palate for good food and wine. Etiquette, as everyone knows, is to refrain from lighting up until the end of the meal. This by no means suits those who pine to enjoy a cigarette in-between whiles and whose pleasure may be curtailed by being denied their foible. It would compound the discourtesy to smoke without asking the host, 'Do you mind?' But as the host is well within bounds to refuse the request, the asker should not be surprised by a negative. Exceptions may well be made in the case of a member whose good-will is being sought or someone to whom special attentions are due.

Experience suggests that the generality of party-givers remain tolerant of smoking but for how long remains a matter of conjecture; keeping cool about the heated topic may rate as one of the social accomplishments of tomorrow. Since hospitality is about ending divisiveness and creating harmony, it is in everyone's interest that these values shouldn't go up in a puff of smoke.

Chief guest

Entertaining the Boss seems to be one of those rites that is set in the tablets. Notwithstanding the possibility that the gender of the host's superior may be female, or that a married male boss may wish to be invited with his girl-friend, ways of attempting to please a guest of honour do not change.

Many bosses have to endure evenings of endless boredom in the cause of business of one kind or another, so the aim is to create an entertaining break from obligation of formality. It would be good if the evening was remembered for friendliness and fun.

The first consideration, as usual, is the guest list. A promising mix might be someone whom the VIP has a special interest in meeting on neutral ground, a person to keep up the party spirit, a familiar face whom he or she is known to like. On the whole, this is not an ideal

*Let's keep it simple or he'll think he pays
me too much.*

opportunity for inviting clever young aspirants who are
likely to try to make their mark by explaining just where
the guest of honour is going wrong.

It is always important to find out what your grandee
likes to eat and drink – especially the latter – and to offer
the favourite. A general guideline on drink is that if the
choice is of plentiful plonk or a measured amount of a
good wine, go for the latter. And if champagne is to be
served to someone with a position in which bubbly flows
with the job, better make it a respectable bottle.

Whatever happens, don't apologise for things not
being as you imagine they are at his or her home – these
probably don't correspond to your imaginings in any
case. Do your best within the resources of the household
and guard against overdoing the aspirational side at all
costs. Punctured pretension is a fail-safe topic for satire.

An opposite number should be found, if possible, for

an unaccompanied guest of honour. But suppose the latter is a woman and no appropriate male can be produced? She may be seated next to one of the partnered males, even if this means that two women will be seated beside one another. At an all-female do at which the usual rules are to be observed, she will be seated on the hostess's right-hand side.

Brushing up

The art of tidying oneself up at table in public requires an insouciant touch as well as an awareness of what might put spectators off their nosh.

Reservations to some extent depend on whether the company is mixed, whether one is in a restaurant or a private domain and the nature of the occasion. Axiomatic is that greater latitude exists in a restaurant.

A general ruling is that light titivation only is acceptable as soon as food comes into the picture. Any action that mistakes a dining table for a dressing table exceeds the limits. For instance, a woman can rearrange her tresses with a deft gesture or two but to embark on purposive brushing and tweaking may destroy an illusion in more ways than one.

Women may check on the state of their make-up whenever they have a will to do so. Applying a fresh lick of lipstick or powdering her nose is par for in-between

My hair is meant to look like this

courses or the end of the meal, as a rule.

The acceptability of using toothpicks in public deserves a word. Despite the argument in favour of periodontic health, it is doubtful if we are ready yet in this country for the practice as part of table manners. An exception might be if these aids are set out on the table, wherever this may be. Producing your own toothpick, though, is taking matters a stage further.

Toothpicks apart, men seem discriminated against as far as the acceptability of grooming in public is concerned. A quick see to the locks and a passing glance in a mirror seem about the limit of what is considered manly in the eyes of most. Manners have yet to adjust to the fact that there is nothing unmanly about a man wishing to attend to his vanities if done with discretion.

Doubts about brushing yourself up are one thing but

what about the dire situation in which your companion is unaware that his or her appearance needs a quick see-to? Whether to make mention of the lipsticky kiss mark on the cheek, or a spinach leaf smile, or a tomato-trickled chin, or a runny nose poses a question mark if the sufferer is anyone other than a friend. Done with grace, the reminder is more than a face-saver. Some manage to get the message across without a word being spoken by pointing a meaningful finger to the spot on their own face that needs attention on that of the observer.

So sorry

Here are two examples of social crises that have lost nothing of their embarrassment, despite the fact that they could happen to anyone.

What do you do if you smash or damage some treasured object in a friend's house? There you are, gesticulating to clinch your point and in a fatal trice you have knocked an Art Deco vase on to the hard floor. There is no way round, except to look as stricken with guilt as you feel. Efforts should be made at once to try to limit the damage and clear up after the debacle. In a party situation, it is important to refrain from allowing the mishap to lower the temperature all round. A stated apology then and there is in order but there is no point in dwelling upon the matter.

*I know we should apologise but I can't
remember what we did.*

Offers to repair or replace the artefact should follow,
assuming the latter is a viable option in terms of cost. A
letter of apology or the prompt dispatch of flowers may
help to mend matters.

What do you do if you are at a party in your Sunday
best and some clumsy nut spills a drink over your attire?
Contingency measures are to take whatever means are
necessary for damage limitation be it salt, milk, water or
sponging. An extremely friendly response is to tell the
spiller that the frock/trousers/jacket was on its way to the
cleaners in any event, and to call the matter a day. It is
infuriating to contemplate the damage but unless there
was any suspicion that the act was not accidental, one
has to rise above it, as they say, in the interests of general
goodwill.

Apologies are due from the perpetrator and an offer
to pay for the dry cleaning – if only as a gesture. As

above, a letter or a bouquet or some token seeking for-giveness would show concern.

Unmentionables

Candour in conversation tends to run dry when a guest wishes to cancel an invitation on grounds that don't bear going into on the telephone. A good example might be a last minute health upset. The position is that not every-one feels comfortable about launching into a graphic description of their ailment – especially if they don't know their host very well – yet politeness calls for a good excuse.

The ideal justification in this case has to convince on the strength of a telling hint of the say-no-more order. Yet, this has to avoid being so circumspect that alarm bells are sounded through omission, rather in the man-ner of hospital bulletins. It is as well, too, that whatever is mentioned should make clear that this is only a tempo-rary indisposition: you don't want people writing in for your job.

Another potential source of embarrassment is that the nature of your disorder may mean you can go about your usual duties whilst at the same time being unfit for socialising. Being unwell doesn't necessarily mean retire-ment from the scene. Yet any excuse given is bound to

*I'm not sure whether to call a taxi
or an ambulance.*

look pretty thin and duplicitous if your host gets word
that you appear to be functioning normally.

The general answer lies in restoring the respectability
of the euphemism: you can have caught the bug that is
going round, or be feeling sick, or have to cut out for a
day or two in the interests of your health. In the instance
of the chucker who is still in circulation it would seem
politic to forestall doubts by offering a hint of the explanation. Everyone is entitled to say they are not completely *hors de combat* but are very poor company.
Other strategies might be a reference to some unpleasant
side effects from the drug to beat the bug, or, a bolder
stroke, an attempt to explain the ailment in medical
jargon that beautifully befuddles the lay listener. Best if
delivered at fast-forward speed that begs no further
questions.

The moules marinière were particularly memorable.

B & B letters

Acknowledging that bread-and-butter letters are as arduous to write as they are pleasurable to receive, the more pertinent issue is how late may you be in sending? The search for an acceptable excuse for tardiness in conveying formal thanks to a host has surely exercised human ingenuity since the days of smoke signals, or so we can safely surmise.

Wild pretexts, 'I've scarcely been able to hold a pen' vie for lack of credibility with such chestnuts as, 'I've just

discovered my original letter behind your photograph.'
Other recognisable pretences of old are scribbling a note
on the back of an sealed envelope implying that the con-
tents were written ages ago, or asking a friend to mail
the missive from remote foreign parts in the hopes the
recipient will blame the delay on the postal services. All
desperado tactics by those who hope to be invited again,
despite the lapse.

A classic redress for belatedness is the penance of
writing a long letter. One sociable jester worked out a
thank-you letter guilt ratio based on half a page of extra
prose to every week of delay, which isn't as silly as it
sounds.

The right length for a thank-you letter is one of the
imponderables and to some extent depends on what is
being thanked for and the writer's degree of indebted-
ness. Also, perhaps, on whether any apologies are due.
Thanks and apologies are epistolary twins.

A letter that comfortably fills a sheet of writing paper
would be fair enough in the usual way of things but it
has to be said that a continuation page does show willing. A few sparse paragraphs only might hint at a lack of
imagination.

The formula, as is well known, is to alight upon some
aspect that convincingly indicates why you had a good
time – bearing in mind the recipient's character, and his
or her reading of yours. Neat grease is not recommended
as it runs the risk of revealing the writer's insincerity.

Ah! I see you two know one another.

Nevertheless, a well-spotted compliment may not come amiss. Possible topics (all else being equal) might be the conversation, the cooking, the choice of wine, the entertainment, the way things were organised, the host's dear ones, and the pleasure of being in their company or that of meeting one or other of the guests. Newcomers to the hearth could mention a warm welcome and being made to feel at home.

Write promptly. Otherwise the old adage applies: it is never too late to send thank-yous. No golds for setting a record.